The Kids Laugh Challenge

Would You Rather?

Valentine's Day Edition

Funny Scenarios, Wacky
Choices and Hilarious Situations
For Kids and Family

With Fun
Illustrations

Be my
valentine

RIDDLELAND

Table of Contents

Riddleland Bonus

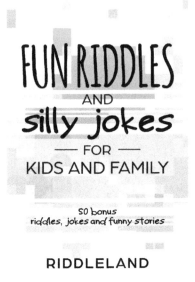

http://pixelfy.me/riddlelandbonus

Thank you for buying this book. We would like to share a special bonus as a token of appreciation. It is a collection of 50 original jokes, riddles, and two super funny stories!

Join our **Facebook Group**
at **Riddleland for Kids** to get
daily jokes and riddles.

Introduction

"All you need is love. But a little chocolate now and then doesn't hurt." ~ **Charles M.Schulz**

We would like to personally thank you for purchasing this book. **Would You Rather? Valentine's Day Edition** is a collection of the funniest scenarios, wacky choices, and hilarious situations for kids and adults to choose from.

These questions are an excellent way to get a conversation started in a fun and exciting way. Also, by asking "Why?" after a "Would you rather" question, you may find interesting answers and learn a lot about a person.

We wrote this book because we want children to be encouraged to read more, think, and grow. As parents, we know that when children play games and learn, they are being educated while having so much fun that they don't even realize they're learning and developing valuable life skills. 'Would you Rather ...' is one of our favorite games to play as a family. Some of the 'would you rather ...' scenarios have had us in fits of giggles, others have generated reactions such as: "Eeeeeeuuugh, that's gross!" and yet others still really make us think and reflect and consider our decisions.

Besides having fun, playing the game also has other benefits such as:

- **Communication** – This game helps children to interact, read aloud, and listen to others. It's a great way to connect. It's a fun way for parents to get their children interacting with them without a formal, awkward conversation. The game can also help to get to know someone better and learn about their likes, dislikes, and values.

- **Builds Confidence** - Children get used to pronouncing vocabulary, asking questions and it helps to deal with shyness.

- **Develops Critical Thinking** – It helps children to defend and justify the rationale for their choices and can generate discussions and debates. Parents playing this game with young children can give them prompting questions about their answers to help them reach logical and sensible decisions.

- **Improves Vocabulary** – Children will be introduced to new words in the questions, and the context of them will help them remember them because the game is fun.

- **Encourages Equality and Diversity** – Considering other people's answers, even if they differ from your own, is important for respect, equality, diversity, tolerance, acceptance, and inclusivity. Some questions may get children to think about options available to them, that don't fall into gendered stereotypes, i.e., careers or activities that challenge the norm.

Would You Rather?
Valentine's Day Edition

How do you play?

At least two players are needed to play this game. Face your opponent and decide who is **Teddy Bear 1** and **Teddy Bear 2**. If you have 3 or 4 players, you can decide which players belong to **Teddy Bear 1** and **Teddy Bear 2**. The goal of the game is to score points by making the other players laugh. The first player to a score of 10 points is the **Round Champion**.

What are the rules?

Teddy Bear 1 starts first. Read the questions aloud and choose an answer. The same player will then explain why they chose the answer in the silliest and wackiest way possible. If the reason makes Teddy Bear 2 laugh, then Teddy Bear 1 scores a funny point. Take turns going back and forth and write down the score.

How do you get started?

Flip a coin. The Teddy Bear that guesses it correctly starts first.

Bonus Tip: Making funny voices, silly dance moves or wacky facial expression will make your opponent laugh!

Most Importantly: Remember to have fun and enjoy the game!

Would You Rather...

Receive a box of chocolates with big bites taken out of every single chocolate OR receive a box of chocolates with all your favorite chocolates missing?

Eat your favorite chocolate off the bottom of your friend's shoe OR receive a Valentine signed by a "secret admirer" and not know who sent it?

Would You Rather...

Spend a whole day dressed up as Cupid, including wearing a diaper as part of the costume OR spend a whole day with a big bright red lipstick kiss mark on your cheek?

Forget all of your classmate's valentines at home on the day of your class party and show up empty-handed OR forget all the valentine candy from your classmates at school after the party and have nothing sweet to eat?

Would You Rather...

Get a licked heart-shaped lollipop stuck in your hair OR get a super sticky chew stuck in between your bare toes?

Get a stinging papercut on each of your fingers from cutting out paper hearts OR have sticky glue covered fingertips that stick to everything for a whole day after you glue together your valentines?

Would You Rather...

Spend all Valentine's Day hugging everyone you meet OR spend all Valentine's Day blowing kisses to everyone you meet?

Have a hole in the bottom of your Valentine's day box and all your Valentine's Day cards fall out on the way home OR have a piece of candy in your Valentine's Day card box melt all over the cards and stick them together?

Would You Rather...

Eat so much Valentine's candy that you get the worst stomach ache ever OR be able to eat as much Valentine's candy as you want to, but you can't taste any after eating two pieces?

Be the kid handing out the candy that no one likes on Valentine's Day OR be the kid with the most popular candy that everyone keeps stealing out of your bag?

Would You Rather...

Get a box of tuna-flavored Valentine's chocolates OR a bunch of lollipops that taste like sour rotten milk?

Say "I Love You Huggy Bear" to everyone on Valentine's Day OR say "Be Mine Divine" to everyone on Valentine's Day?

Would You Rather...

Shoot rubber arrows at people like Cupid does to make them fall in love OR leave random love notes hidden all over a park or playground?

Have fingers that are sticky lollipops that have already been licked all over OR toes made from Valentine's chocolates that melt in your socks and shoes?

15

Would You Rather...

Cut out your valentines with fingers that
work as a pair of super snappy scissors
OR glue them with a nose that works as
a gloopy glue bottle?

Wear a shirt that says, "My mommy loves me
most" OR wear a shirt that says, "I love my
mommy THIS much!" all day long?

Would You Rather...

Make sloppy Valentine's cards that never look quite like hearts OR write so messy on the cards that no one can read them?

Have pink and red hearts drawn all over your face that won't wash off for two days OR only be able to draw hearts instead of any letters for two whole days?

Would You Rather...

Walk around school with a Valentine's card stuck to the bottom of your shoe all day OR with heartshaped Valentine's erasers stuck on all ten of your fingers?

Get a love letter from last Valentine's Day in the mail today OR send a love letter that never gets delivered?

Would You Rather...

Find a melted chocolate heart in your belly button OR one completely melted under your armpit?

Be able to shoot red paper hearts from your mouth OR cry tears of yummy milk chocolate?

Would You Rather...

Have the only valentine gift you get be from your parents on Valentine's Day OR wake up buried in a pile of random valentines?

Eat a box of Valentine's candy filled with chocolate covered mushrooms OR eat a Valentine's lunch that is a bowl of lettuce covered with chocolate sauce instead of salad dressing?

Would You Rather...

Get caught passing love notes in class and your face turns beet red OR spill a glass of red fruit punch all over your clean white shirt?

Fall in love with your reflection in the mirror and name yourself "Honeybunch" OR fall in love with a pet rock named "Pebbles" who goes with you everywhere?

Would You Rather...

Take a relaxing bath in a tub full of floating heartshaped candles OR take a nap snuggled up to the person you love most?

Be a lonely mailman or woman delivering everyone else's valentines in the mail OR stand all day by your mailbox waiting for the mailman or woman to come and then get no valentines in the mail?

Would You Rather...

Have hot hands that melt every piece of Valentine's chocolate you try to eat OR have ice cold hands that freeze your chocolates rock hard?

Have "sticky hug hands" that get stuck to anyone you hug OR push away from anyone you try to hug like an opposing magnet?

Would You Rather...

Style your hair for Valentine's Day using melted chocolate OR wear an outfit made completely out of chocolate which can melt if you get too warm?

Exchange valentines with kids that are two years older than you OR exchange valentines with kids that are two years younger than you?

Would You Rather...

Find a hidden valentine in your cereal box after it falls into your bowl of milk OR find a hidden valentine on the floor of your shower after you've turned on the water?

Do your homework only using words on conversation heart candies OR only be able to say words and phrases that come from Valentine's Day greeting cards?

Would You Rather...

Make your own homemade valentines using glitter, glue, and scissors OR spend three hours shopping with your dad and buying valentines at the store?

Think that you have the ugliest Valentine's box in your class but it's very sturdy OR the coolest box, but it falls completely apart when the first valentine is put in the box?

Would You Rather...

Spend a whole day hiding in a giant heart-shaped Valentine's box OR be flattened in between a giant Valentine's Day card?

Be the star of a romantic play where everyone falls in love with you OR sing a song that makes everyone get googly lovey eyes every time you sing a note?

Would You Rather...

Have a heart-shaped head and never been able to wear a hat again OR have heart-shaped feet so you have to walk around barefoot all the time?

Have eyes that are shaped like pretty little hearts OR be able to blow heart-shaped bubbles out of your belly button?

Would You Rather...

Have pretty pink hearts painted on all of your fingernails OR have rosy red hearts on every single one of your teeth?

Sleep in a heart-shaped bed surrounded by heartshaped pillows OR only be able to wear clothes that are covered in red, pink, and white hearts for a week straight?

Would You Rather...

Sing mushy love songs loud and proud every time you take a shower OR write love notes to yourself on the steamy mirror every time you take a shower?

Fall in love with a mouse that you find hiding in your house and declare that he's your one true love OR never fall in love your whole life long?

Would You Rather...

Eat a giant stack of 10 huge heart-shaped pancakes completely covered in sticky maple syrup OR eat just one paper Valentine's card covered in chocolate?

Have someone fall madly in puppy love with you, sending you love notes all the time and following you around OR be the one who falls madly in puppy love with someone else and sends them love notes and follows them around all the time?

Would You Rather...

Play a game of tic-tac-toe using only hearts - no x's or o's OR complete a jumbo word search by drawing hearts around all the words instead of circling them?

Bake heart-shaped chocolate chip cookies for all your friends OR get an empty valentine's candy box on your doorstep?

Would You Rather...

Eat a heart-shaped lollipop and get it stuck all over your teeth before having your picture taken OR go to school with a heart-shaped hole in the seat of your pants?

Drink everything from a heart-shaped straw for one whole month OR eat only heart-shaped strawberries every meal for one week straight?

Drink a cup of bright red hot chocolate OR eat a five pound bar of ruby red chocolate in one sitting?

Carry a hot pink teddy bear around with you wherever you go for a week OR wear only a shirt that says "I love my daddy the most" every day for a week?

Would You Rather...

Send a love note to your dog every day that he just eats and drools on OR get love notes from your cat which are scratched into your couch?

Swim in a pool full of pink water that dyes everything it touches pink OR wake up to your mom standing over your bed singing a song about how much she loves you?

Would You Rather...

Have hearts flying out of your head whenever you're around someone you really like OR leave heartshaped footprints everywhere you walk?

Take a terrifying ride on a heart-shaped rollercoaster OR ride right next to your crush on the ghost train?

Would You Rather...

Take a bath in a heart-shaped bathtub filled with pink bubbles OR wash your hair with neon pink shampoo and conditioner?

Walk around with a heart-shaped frame around your face all the time OR be driven around in a ruby red heart-shaped car?

Would You Rather...

Carry a mirror with you and kiss it every five minutes OR walk around all day giving yourself a big old bear hug?

Get a box of Valentine's Day chocolates that tastes like you're eating vegetables OR use a giant milk chocolate heart as your pillow at night?

Would You Rather...

Take a bath in a tub filled with red rose petals OR sleep on a pillowcase filled with fragrant red rose petals?

Prick your finger on the thorn of a rose every day before bed OR try to smell the roses every morning and get stung by a bee?

Would You Rather...

Do all of your homework for a week using a Valentine's Day pencil made completely from chocolate OR try to fix a piece of writing by using a pencil with a heart-shaped eraser made from chocolate?

Pluck petals from daisies all day saying "he/she loves me not...he/she loves me" OR wear perfume or cologne made from really smelly daisies for a whole day?

Would You Rather...

Carry around a basket of roses to give to people and be called "flower girl" or "flower boy" OR have random people throw rose petals in front of you wherever you walk?

Play in a sandbox filled with conversation hearts instead of sand OR get a whole box of assorted valentine's chocolate candies but only be able to take one bite out of each candy?

Would You Rather...

Replace all the zeros on your math work with hearts OR sign your name with a cute little heart at the end of it?

Be unable to stop yourself from ending every conversation with "Later gorgeous" OR begin every conversation with "Hey handsome"?

Would You Rather...

Be caught holding hands with your grandma at the shopping mall OR caught holding hands with your grandpa at a baseball game?

Sleep on a bed made from thorny roses OR pick a dozen thorny roses with your bare hands?

Would You Rather...

Celebrate Valentine's Day with chocolate, hearts, and flowers every day for the whole month of February OR celebrate Halloween by trick-or-treating every day for the whole month of October?

Play for an hour in a giant ball pit filled with tiny conversation hearts OR play a game of dodgeball with your friends using conversation hearts instead of balls?

Would You Rather...

Sit outside your sibling's bedroom window singing love songs and playing a guitar OR have your mom or dad sitting outside your window loudly singing you love songs while playing a guitar?

Agree with everything everyone says by saying "Love it, darling" OR disagree with everything everyone says by saying "I just don't love it"?

Would You Rather...

Get a beautiful bouquet of flowers that makes you sneeze every time you are near it OR get a beautiful bouquet of flowers that is covered in ants?

Go to a Valentine's Day party and play pin the kissy on the lips OR play a game of Truth or Dare: hug edition?

Would You Rather...

Fill your entire room with paper chains of hearts OR carry a bag full of confetti wherever you go, throwing little handfuls into the air over your head?

Be dropped off at school in front of your classmates by your mom who gives you a big sloppy wet kiss OR be dropped off at school by your mom who yells at you out the car window, "Love you sweetums"?

Would You Rather...

Work in a bakery being the person who gets to decorate and frost all of the heart-shaped sugar cookies OR have the easy, but messy job of being the person who gets to shake colorful sprinkles on all of the decorated cookies?

Drink a jumbo cup of hot chocolate filled with floating conversation hearts OR wear an outfit that has conversation hearts glued ALL OVER it?

Would You Rather...

Eat a giant heart-shaped chocolate donut filled with strawberry jam OR eat a giant heart-shaped strawberry donut filled with chocolate pudding?

Have your little sibling run up to you on the playground every day and call you "Snookums" OR have your favorite (but embarrassing) stuffed animal accidentally fall out of your backpack where everyone can see it?

Would You Rather...

Have a large red heart-shaped birthmark on the middle of your forehead OR have a heart-shaped nose sitting right in the middle of your face?

Wear an entire armful of conversation heart bracelets that you have to eat in less than five minutes OR wear an entire armful of conversation heart bracelets that people keep trying to take a bite from for a whole day?

Would You Rather...

Paint your bedroom bright pink with red and white hearts all over it, including the ceiling OR paint your classroom bright pink with red and white hearts all over everything, including your desk?

Wear rose colored glasses and see only the good in things all the time OR be suspicious of anything and everything all the time?

Would You Rather...

Sit in a heart-shaped desk chair that doesn't properly fit your bottom OR wear a pair of jeans that has a big red heart on the seat of the pants?

Write the most awesome love letter which is guaranteed to make anyone fall in love with you but then be too chicken to send it OR sing the most gushy love song to someone you love and have your voice croak loudly right at the best part?

Would You Rather...

Eat a bag full of pink and red heart-shaped potato chips OR eat a cute little pizza which is in the shape of a heart with heart-shaped pepperonis on it?

Try to bowl a perfect 13 strike 300 game with a heart-shaped bowling ball OR try to swish a halfcourt basketball shot with a heart-shaped basketball?

Would You Rather...

Lick a heart-shaped lollipop that fell on the floor and is now covered in cat hair OR eat a chocolate chip cookie that fell into your dog's water bowl?

Be made completely out of red heart-shaped glitter, leaving little sparkly tracks wherever you go OR leave little heart-shaped handprints on everything you touch?

Would You Rather...

Eat a candlelit dinner with your mom and dad on Valentine's Day OR go to the movies with your grandma and grandpa with you sitting right between them?

Be bitten by a lovebug and fall in love with anything and everything OR be bitten by a stink bug and smell bad all the time?

Would You Rather...

Have your little brother or sister run up to you on the playground and give you a giant sloppy wet kiss on the cheek OR have your little brother or sister come up to your classroom because they wet their pants?

Eat a bowl of super cheesy heart-shaped macaroni and cheese noodles OR have your mom cut all your sandwiches into heart shapes?

Would You Rather...

Walk around school all day with a heart-shaped Valentine's Day lollipop stuck to the back of your pants OR walk around school all day with melted chocolate Valentine's heart smeared on the back of your pants?

Get a huge box full of classroom valentines filled with opened and eaten candy OR only get two valentines that have your favorite candy attached?

Would You Rather...

Wear a pink paper heart crown for a whole day OR wear a pair of hot pink heart-shaped sunglasses for a whole day?

Be forced to take your teacher a giant box of chocolates on Valentine's Day OR be forced to bring your teacher a giant bunch of flowers on Valentine's Day?

Would You Rather...

Only be able to do your homework in red and pink markers for all of Valentine's Day week OR have your fingernails and toenails painted pink and red for all of February?

Eat a giant stack of raspberry-flavored heartshaped pancakes covered in thick, sweet raspberry syrup OR eat an entire chocolate lava cake that is filled with a tart raspberry filling?

Would You Rather...

Receive a love letter that is written in a different language so you can't understand it OR receive a love letter written in the sand on the beach?

Have a hole in the back of your pants and bright pink underwear showing through OR drop a note out of your pocket that someone finds and reads to the whole class, "I love you pinkie pie - Mom"?

Would You Rather...

Have a pencil box filled with heart-shaped pencils that hurt your hands to hold OR have red heartshaped freckles all over your face?

Ride all the way to your friend's house on a bicycle that has streamers with glittery hearts hanging off the handlebars OR try to ride to school on a skateboard with heart-shaped wheels?

Would You Rather...

Trade all your Valentine's candy with your little brother or sister OR have to tag along on a Valentine's date with your big brother or sister on Valentine's Day?

Spend an afternoon floating on a giant bubblegum pink heart-shaped pool float OR go swimming with your friends wearing little heart-shaped arm floaties?

Would You Rather...

Have your face stuck in a fish lips face for a whole day, like you're just about to kiss someone OR have the feeling that someone has just planted a big wet and sloppy kiss on your cheek for a whole day?

Only be able to say things from conversation heart candies like "B Mine" OR eat a whole spinach-flavored heart lollipop?

Have a pet dog who writes you love poetry OR have a pet cat who presents you with heart-shaped hairballs?

Wear a sign on your back that says "Love Muffin" for a whole day OR a sign on your forehead that says "Kiss Me" for one hour?

Would You Rather...

Fall in love with doing homework and spend all your free time doing it OR fall in love with bug collecting and spend your days with your little creepy crawly love bugs?

Receive a box full of valentines that are all written backwards and need to be read in a mirror OR receive a box full of valentines that are all written upside down and need to be read while standing on your head?

Would You Rather...

Wear a shirt with red and pink hearts all over it OR wear pants with pictures of cupid all over them?

Eat a delicious looking chocolate that has a not so delicious dirt filling inside OR eat a heart-shaped donut dusted with sand from your sandbox?

Would You Rather...

Receive a bunch of beautiful flowers that smell wonderful OR a giant box of delicious looking chocolates that don't taste very good for Valentine's Day?

Not have a class Valentine's party on Valentine's Day OR have a class Halloween party where you only get candy that you absolutely hate?

Would You Rather...

Get a silly Valentine's Day card that makes you laugh so hard that you snort OR get a super sappy Valentine's Day card that makes you cry?

Drink a love potion that is colored black but tastes perfectly fruity OR drink a love potion and not fall in love with anyone afterwards?

Would You Rather...

Listen to your teacher reading a love story for story time every day for a week OR spend your free time during class cutting out Valentine's hearts for your classmates?

Read a love poem out loud in front of your whole class OR have someone read a love poem out loud to you in front of the whole class?

Would You Rather...

Have armpits that smell like a bunch of roses OR feet that smell like your favorite chocolate bar?

Eat a chocolate-covered cherry that oozes cream all down your chin OR bite into a chocolate covered caramel that leaves caramel stuck all over your teeth?

Would You Rather...

Show up to school and see your Principal dressed up as Cupid, carrying around a fake bow and arrow OR dressed as Santa Claus, with a pillow for a belly and a big white fake beard?

Have a birthday on Valentine's Day and all you ever get is a big box of chocolate OR have your birthday on Christmas and get a giant frosted sugar cookie instead of a cake?

Would You Rather...

Be a wedding photographer always taking pictures of people in love OR be a baby photographer always taking pictures of children crying?

Catch your parents kissing each other every time you walk into the room OR get hugged by your parents every time you walk into the room?

Would You Rather...

Wear a shirt that says, "Kiss Me" OR a shirt that says "Ask me for a hug" on Valentine's Day?

Wear shoes made from bouncy rubbery red gummy hearts OR wear shoes made from sticky pink bubble gum?

Would You Rather...

Try to make a batch of heart-shaped pancakes for breakfast OR eat heart-shaped tuna sandwiches for lunch on Valentine's Day?

Wake up one morning with skin that is completely Valentine's red from head to toe OR wake up one morning with hair that has turned bright bubblegum pink?

Would You Rather...

Eat a candlelit dinner of hamburgers and fries with your parents for Valentine's Day OR spend the night eating popcorn on the couch and watching movies with a few friends?

Accidentally send an "I luv u" text to your best friend instead of your mom OR get an "I luv u" text from your friend with no explanation as to why?

Would You Rather...

Play a game of kickball using a heart-shaped ball that rolls in a wonky way across the ground OR play a game of tennis using a large heart-shaped racquet?

Use your teeth to bite a bunch of heart shapes into red construction paper OR use chewed bubble gum to glue together a paper heart chain?

Would You Rather...

Cook a special Valentine's dinner by making all the food into the shape of hearts OR wear a special Valentine's Day outfit that is made completely out of hearts?

Marry your best friend and always get along without having disagreements OR marry your true love and fight like cats and dogs about every silly little thing?

Would You Rather...

Try to eat a bowl of chicken noodle soup with a heart-shaped spoon OR try to drink a cup of chocolate milk out of a heart-shaped cup?

Have a heartbeat that sounds like a cow mooing OR moo like a cow whenever someone gives you a hug or a kiss?

Would You Rather...

Have a Valentine's bake-off with your best friend making heart-shaped chocolate chip cookies OR miniature heart-shaped cherry cheesecakes?

Have a curly hairdo that is cut into the shape of a heart OR have a bunch of tiny hearts shaved into your head?

Would You Rather...

Go to an art studio and paint a Valentine's Day portrait of you and your best friend OR go to a photo studio with your friend and take a photo with a bunch of silly heart and cupid props?

Be a famous filmmaker known for love stories guaranteed to make you cry OR be a famous singer whose voice makes people fall in love?

Would You Rather...

Give your grandma the Valentine's gift of a facial with face-pack and cucumber slices over the eyes OR give your grandpa the Valentine's gift of a pedicure?

Lose your ability to taste sweet food so you no longer enjoy chocolate, candy, or bubble gum OR lose your ability to taste salty food, so potato chips and pretzels are just crunchy things in your mouth?

Would You Rather...

Be served a lovely Valentine's breakfast
in bed of chocolate-dipped strawberries
OR chocolate-dipped French toast?

Get a love letter that is torn in half and
missing the bottom half OR watch a love story
on TV and miss the last 30 minutes?

Would You Rather...

Cook your parents a special Valentine's dinner all by yourself OR eat a four course Valentine's meal cooked for you by using only your hands?

Use a crayon box that only has different shades of red, pink, and white OR have heart-shaped erasers on all your pencils?

Would You Rather...

Write someone a love letter using red fingerpaint OR write the love letter using chocolate pudding?

Have to finish a 500-piece puzzle made entirely from heart-shaped pieces OR put together a giant heart-shaped puzzle where all of the pieces are exactly the same shade of red?

Would You Rather...

Spend Valentine's Day babysitting your younger sibling(s) so your parents can go on a date OR spend Valentine's Day getting beaten at board games by your family?

Wear a sash that says "Most loveable" to school every day for a week OR wear the same t-shirt that says "I love hugs" to school every day?

Would You Rather...

Go to a trampoline park and jump on pink heart-shaped trampolines OR spend an afternoon jumping in a giant red heart-shaped bouncy house?

Wear a shirt that says, "Love is for losers" and spend the entire Valentine's Day by yourself OR a shirt that says "Love is for puppies" and spend your day in a house with twenty puppies?

Would You Rather...

Bend a bunch of jumbo paper clips into heart shapes OR crumple a bunch of pieces of aluminum foil into valentine's hearts?

Eat a giant hot fudge sundae topped with a big red cherry on top OR eat a giant bowl of sweet fluffy whipped cream with a big red cherry on top?

Would You Rather...

Make valentine hearts using string and a bottle of glue OR cut out paper valentine hearts using scissors covered in sticky stuff?

Go see a very loud concert with someone you really like, but it's so loud you can't talk to each other OR agree to go to a restaurant that serves food you don't like at all because the person you like wants to go there?

Would You Rather...

Bake heart-shaped cakes and chocolates
OR just buy some from the store

Share a Valentine's dance with your mom
who hugs you closely and cries a little while
you dance OR with your dad who awkwardly
wiggles and jiggles while trying to bust out
some cool moves?

Would You Rather...

Not have homework for the day OR receive a gift from all your classmates?

Have a Valentine's slumber party with your best friend where you paint nails and style your hair together OR a slumber party where you try on different clothes and put on a fashion show?

Would You Rather...

Dress up as Cupid for a party OR the Queen of Hearts?

Not be able to kiss your parents but hug them all you want OR not be able to hug your parents but kiss them all you want for the rest of your life?

Would You Rather...

Wear large heart shape sunglasses OR a tall heart shape top hat to school?

Go ice skating with your crush and hold hands while trying not to fall on your butt OR go sledding and ride in the same sled with your crush trying not to fall out of the sled?

Would You Rather...

Swim in a pool filled with rose petals OR red balloons?

Eat Valentine's dinner at a super fancy restaurant and choose what to eat from a menu of food that you've never heard of before OR go to a posh concert and spend two hours listening to music that you've never heard before?

Would You Rather...

Paint your face red with hearts OR
color your hair red?

Get to act in a special Valentine's
episode of your favorite TV show OR
write the script for it?

Would You Rather...

Have a magic carpet OR an invisibility cloak as a gift for Valentine's Day?

Go for a hot air balloon ride OR ride boats under the Tunnel of Love in Venice?

Would You Rather...

Get shot by Cupid's arrow OR avoid it?

Receive 100 Valentine's cards through your letterbox from friends OR receive just one special Valentine's card from a secret admirer?

Would You Rather...

Approach new people and talk to them OR have them approach you?

Find a picture of yourself with your face circled in hearts and kisses laying in the middle of the hall OR find a bunch of red roses stuffed into your backpack with a note saying "Love ?"?

Would You Rather...

Celebrate Valentine's Day by having a picnic near the river OR for a bicycle ride?

Hear the sound of your heart beating slowly every time you lay in bed trying to fall asleep OR hear your heartbeat thumping in your chest every time you are moving your body?

Would You Rather...

Go to watch a zombie movie starring your best friend OR a romantic one?

Receive a bunch of mushy gushy love notes meant for someone else OR drop your valentines on the ground and watch them all blow away in the wind?

Would You Rather...

Receive a surprise Valentine's package in your school locker OR receive a gift that you were expecting?

The hiccups in front of your crush OR burp in front of the class?

Would You Rather...

Swim in the ocean with a mermaid OR fly
through the air with Cupid?

Receive Valentine's from people all over
the world OR just receive one from your
favorite singer?

101

Would You Rather...

Write a love letter to a pen pal you've never met OR to a classmate that you sit beside every day?

A horse gives you a slobbery Valentine's kiss on the cheek OR an elephant?

Would You Rather...

Go to lunch with Harry Potter OR
Ron Weasley on Valentine's Day?

Pay someone $10, plus the cost of dinner, to
go on a date for you OR get paid $10 and
get a free dinner to go on a date for
someone else?

Would You Rather...

Fly a heart-shaped kite OR be a heart-shaped kite?

Find your forever true love but lose your ability to speak for the rest of your life OR spend your life traveling the world looking for true love and never finding it?

Would You Rather...

Be given heart-shaped balloons OR a heart-shaped cake?

End every conversation on Valentine's Day with "I wuv you" OR begin every conversation on Halloween with "smell my feet"?

Would You Rather...

Eat red popcorn for the entire day
OR take a walk-in red rain?

Deliver homemade valentine's to older
people living in nursing homes to brighten
their days OR deliver boxes of chocolate
hearts to people who are in the hospital
on Valentine's Day?

Would You Rather...

Have a unicorn horn appear on your head throughout all of January OR have angel wings appear on your back just on Valentine's Day?

Live in a house that is painted the hottest shade of hot pink OR live in a house that has red windows which make everything inside looks pink?

Would You Rather...

Receive a huge teddy bear as a gift OR a big box of chocolates?

Begin every sentence with "Roses are red, the sky is blue..." OR end every sentence "sugar is sweet, and so are you"?

Did you enjoy the book?

If you did, we are ecstatic. If not, please write your complaint to us and we will ensure to fix it.

If you're feeling generous, there is something important that you can help me with – tell other people that you enjoyed the book.

Ask a grown-up to write about it on Amazon. When they do, more people will find out about the book. It also lets Amazon know that we are making kids around the world laugh. Even a few words and ratings would go a long way.

If you have any ideas or jokes that you think are super funny, please let us know. We would love to hear from you. Our email address is - **riddleland@riddlelandforkids.com**

Riddleland Bonus

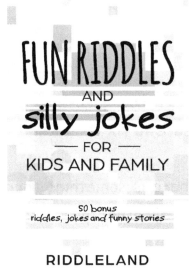

http://pixelfy.me/riddlelandbonus

Thank you for buying this book. We would like to share a special bonus as a token of appreciation. It is a collection of 50 original jokes, riddles, and two super funny stories!

Join our **Facebook Group**
at **Riddleland for Kids** to get
daily jokes and riddles.

Would you like your jokes and riddles to be featured in our next book?

We are having a contest to see who are the smartest or funniest boys and girls in the world! :
1) **Creative and Challenging Riddles**
2) **Tickle Your Funny Bone Contest**

Parents, please email us your child's "Original" Riddle or Joke and **he or she could win a $25 Amazon gift card and be featured in our next book.**

Here are the rules:
1) We're looking for super challenging riddles and extra funny jokes.
2) Jokes and riddles MUST be 100% original—NOT something discovered on the Internet.
3) You can submit both a joke and a riddle because they are two separate contests.
4) Don't get help from your parents—unless they're as funny as you are.
5) Winners will be announced via email or our Facebook group – Riddleland for Kids
6) In your entry, please confirm which book you purchased.
7) Email us at Riddleland@riddlelandforkids.com

Other Fun Children Books for Kids!

Riddles Series

The Laugh Challenge Series

Would You Rather... Series

Get them on Amazon
or our website at www.riddlelandforkids.com

About Riddleland

Riddleland is a mom + dad run publishing company. We are passionate about creating fun and innovative books to help children develop their reading skills and fall in love with reading. If you have suggestions for us or want to work with us, shoot us an email at riddleland@riddlelandforkids.com

Our family's favorite quote:

"Creativity is an area in which younger people have a tremendous advantage since they have an endearing habit of always questioning past wisdom and authority."
~ Bill Hewlett

Made in the USA
Middletown, DE
11 February 2021